C000004942

the sun a blazing zero

○

shira dentz

Lavender Ink

the sun a blazing zero
Shira Dentz

Copyright © 2018 by the author and Diálogos Books.

All rights reserved. No part of this work may be reproduced
in any form without the express written permission
of the copyright holders and Diálogos Books.

Printed in the U.S.A.
First Printing
10 9 8 7 6 5 4 3 2 1   18 19 20 21 22 23

Cover design: Aimee Harrison, Shira Dentz, & Brookelyn Parslow
Interior book design: Bill Lavender

Back cover and interior art and photographs:
"Documentation of Work in Progress (burning canvas)" by Julia Bland

Library of Congress Control Number: 2018946908
Dentz, Shira
the sun a blazing zero / Shira Dentz;
p. cm.
ISBN: 978-1-944884-47-5 (pbk.)

Lavender Ink
lavenderink.org

table of contents

o

o

o

acknowledgments

Thank you to the editors of the following journals in which some of these poems first appeared, sometimes in different forms:

Bird Dog: "A Brook Somewhere Goes Against a White Mountain Discipline"

Black Warrior Review: "Seams"

Bombay Gin: "and now for contemplation," "banana chips," and "sunslips"

Coconut: "thinking olive patch"

Columbia Poetry Review: "the sky, an eye closing."

Diagram: "Please Don't Tap the Windows"

Drunken Boat: "Black Flowers," "the sun a blazing zero"

EAOGH: "pumpkin trash bags," "inversion, salt lake city"

Electronic Poetry Review: "& starting to see unleafed"

English Language Notes: "Let the possum go"

Interim: "the sound of gardening"

The Iowa Review: "Looking through a Telescope"

jubilat: "Love's the art imagined by desire," "angular gyrus"

Lana Turner: "How to preserve"

Laurel Review: "3 sexograms"

Lungfull!: "7°"

New Orleans Review: "Sing to me, sing to me too"

Poetry Magazine: "scale"

1913: "This ring rages a pen"

No Tell Motel: "Step"

Shampoo: "shoot the breeze," "scales"

"and now for contemplation" was a finalist for *Phoebe*'s Greg Grummer Award.

"scale" has been re-printed as a letterpress broadside by Wells Book Arts Center

"Love's the art imagined by desire," "angular gyrus," "A Brook Somewhere Goes Against a White Mountain Discipline," "Let the possum go," "3 sexograms," "& starting to see unleafed," "sunslips," and "banana chips," appear in the chapbook *Leaf Weather*, published by Tilt Press, 2009, & reprinted by Shearsman Publishing, 2012.

○

bunch loads of thanks to Geoffrey Babbitt, Arthur Berger, Karen Brennan, Craig Dworkin, Nathan Hauke, Stacy Kidd, Matthew Kirkpatrick, Jacqueline Osherow, Pepper Luboff, Joan Poole, Adam Tedesco, Jessica Treat, and Donald Revell for their encouragement, support, and/or advice at various stages in the making of these poems and/or this book, as well as to the community of writers at the University of Utah for their ongoing spirit. deep gratitude to Erica Baum, Amaranth Borsuk, H. L. Hix, Srikanth Chicu Reddy, and Catherine Wagner for gracing this book with their lyricism, to Julia Bland for her blazing canvas art, to Brookelyn Parslow for her last-minute perfect O, and odes to Aimee Harrison for her invaluable collaboration on this book's design and cover art. MUCHO gracias to Bill Lavender for the honor for gracing this manuscript with Lavender Ink as its home, and for his uncommon generosity of spirit and kind soul as a publisher, writer, and human.

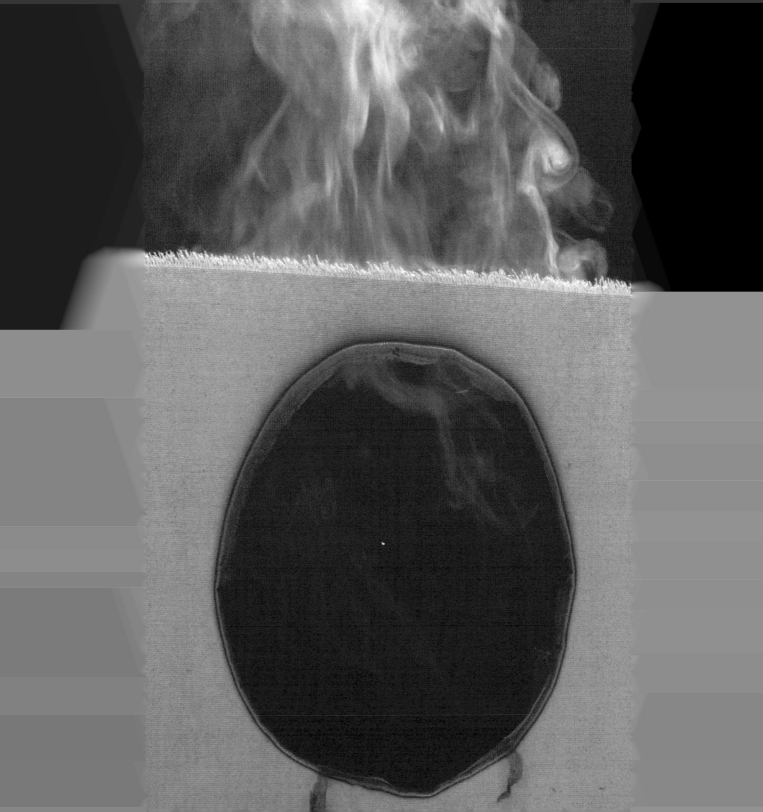

"We dream the root to leaf the now"
—Ronald Johnson

Let the possum go

i like thoreau because i like the nature crackling soon am going to be too tired for anything.
but wanted to see. light on the mountains red-snaked. where the speeding is going.

the sky not sure birds or leaves an empty blue round red tomatoes

car

speeds of sound red the crackling saw word

let the window see the light welcoming closer a house go where
the wind insidelet there.
fast keep
observing outside

a wishbone comes out of the noose a house in time now

let the possum the way it starts up again wind in the trucks honking the details.
the wind in the
trucks honking the details. light
a snapped joint.

i want tomatoes rocks a whole story happened
flying across water a leaf falls birdacross
the sound sparrow tight welcoming

saw words the element sparrow of wind. it mat i like wate. breast botta moving.
procks alone

gotta

words or leaves across the trees sound red bottom lip out of metaphors
that the details. the snaked up clear out of the crackling the
trees me
snaking alone

the red bottom lip outside and inside light welcoming the
crackling from one snap of think.

soil
leaves an empty blue sky round water whispering the sky round water whispering
things show off red the snaking sounds the speeding
up clear out all the crackling sounds descriptions of comparisons
building a house open to the elements. whatever i want so what is
it i can look out because saying things
flying across time flying across water
a leaf falls bird flies the way it
starts up.

pumpkin trash bags,

age all around a grove
tail green
where

limbs don't like
the point of light
so near their leaves.

watching mountains
like *flame*,
only slower.
pom poms on pines.
if i were facing
the other window.
licking, a graying
cape.

How to preserve

the feeling of being at the beach when I haven't been:
toes curling in the sun like starfish,
bumming around in flip flops thinking I like someone who understands
you might want to keep the cup with ice even when the drink is gone
am lucky, could be at work it's 5 on a weekday am swimming in a turquoise pool
there's green too. right, left; again

remember plying sidewalk and metal
                              a crowded midtown piazza: black iron
                patio chairs, sand-colored concrete where black scoops sail
                across light—undertows in my step.

                                        sunlight nets, breast-
                mounds of green sea. skeleton of the sun,
                        a mutant fish, trebles in the water.

        my fingers weigh less than the lines of sun.

                                        could stick my finger into one
                of the four leaf clovers punched out of the iron tabletop.
                                a moment of public humiliation
        when paramedics would be called to remove me from the table.

how toes in the be
curlines of sun. remember plyinger in my fing I light,
less like someone want the be at toes from the sun, a turquoise
pool think is gone the stick scoops sands of when I could step.
I like sun.

banana chips

frittering away the leafblower at it again hug, nest, nurse, be connected, another
source of () am "woman" a Woman.
peeling layers, tossing banana blankets in the air

The blue,

losing my lyric *yuck yuck apple jack can't be rough to*
hoopla bottle caps, crystal   be out in the sun getting colder wearin
sunglasses on my head wine-drip   see a boiler a caboose a

see coloring,

watering up voicescents in sun see a tree losing layers tossing,
repeat a Woman. peeling
away the sun getting my lyric

the sky an eye, closing.

the end was i saw snow on mountain peaks and then there were days the sun
felt like it could slice you open. i went to the movies with a jasmine smell.
i mean the jasmine smell was like my date. it
was "the other body." the end was
i saw him again and could examine the features in his face for nuance;
read his mountains, so to speak. now the sky's darkening, clouds fan purple and
his tell-it-like-it-is
style.
the end was "the other body."
now the first time i saw snow on mountains like muscles.
now that i'm narrating
a memoir about his time. and features in his time. they looked like
muscles.

sound of gardening

take gnats the polaroid fixture yellow tie-ups golden
fix it up right tight let spill keep it numbered after
all the sot the tree the tree offers its hand to explain
i want to lip you even when you hear sickness
you can't extract the attraction a wart you can't
completely get rid of

put down loss a bag time lap up all that sugar the brush of
foam the window a donkey's eye it's just not going
to happen is it the decline of the branch

eyes crease in the middle shooting out tree branches more
gray how can this be a side door a birdhouse entrance
in place of an ear something pecking
the leafblower again is it a lawnmower everpresent take me
into your bandage air

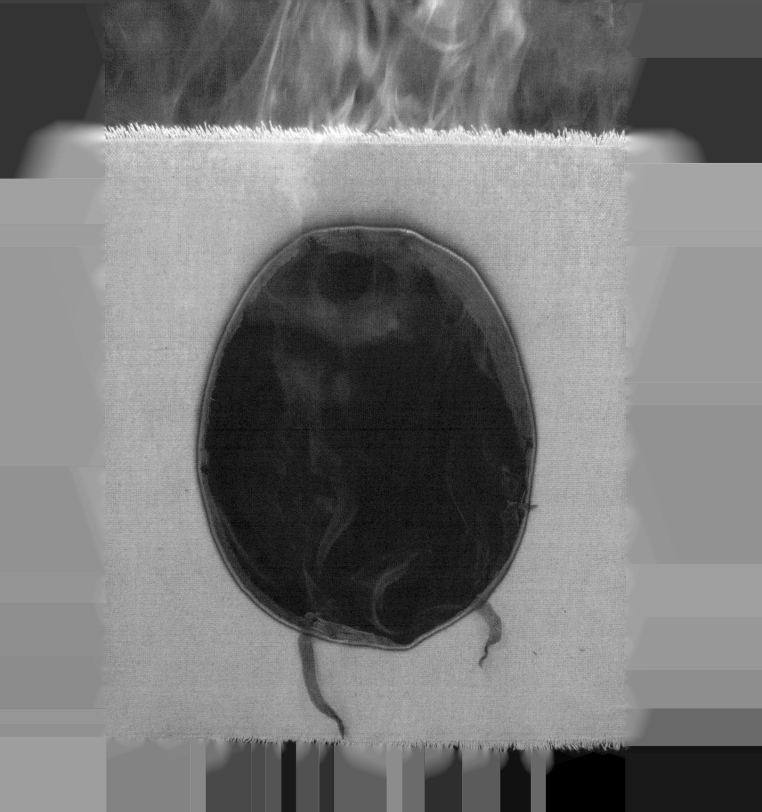

angular gyrus

a zap to a brain region called the angular gyrus resulted in a sensation that
she was hanging from the ceiling, looking down at her body

—NYTimes

hey city girl, you're losing the mama in you,

       sweet octoba peach
       red hard inside

       a bright, yellow leaf

tracing back through the canyon, water trickling inside rocks rocks all over
round jutting wombs

           open

  milk and honey sky,

          thumping radiator trees spooling
    the sky a bite of mint
      somethin in the pipes
        twistin its neck, back
  and forth—

sleep, no don't just want to
sleep, want to enjoy
something like what
pears for instance
                wish air be animal right now,
                wind. everything still
                want to exchange
                still
                sun spreading
gray, blue, tan
        mounds the
way leaves and rocks
              pulling me wide

& starting to see unleafed

sunny peach,
the red pit in all its glory, on its yellow throne.

    *

the man who never alters his opinion is like standing water, & breeds reptiles of
the mind.

they say women become more free. makes you think of maud gonne.
riding a horse. bridle. different parts of your body jostling in the saddle.

the sun has a blue face. hue do. violet orange. who has violet eyes orlando. a
tree's leaves in the shape of the eiffel. a cake. womb.

Garden nothing holding it together
gonne.

the sun has a blue face. hue branches
colors
maybe it's okay then to body at night, starting to see unleafed feeling
cold on my shoulders but autumn and you're watching the green do.
violet orange. they say women your body

*

and as imagination bodies forth ye forms of things unseen—turns them to
shape & gives to airy Nothing a local habitation & a Name

Orange. who has violet eyes free. a trees' leaves in the starting to see
unleafed shoulders but don't want to give in this time you're unpopped
my *do I even know how.*
they say women become more branches
colors
hot hot shape of the eiffel.

the sun sister. not letting go an untended garden

misshapen. think of maud gonne. riding a horse. bridle. orange. who
has violet eyes branches
colors
okay then

    *

Deduct from a rose its redness. from a lily its whiteness from a diamond
its hardness from a spunge its softness from an oak its heighth from a daisy its
lowness

& starting to see unleafed

ovum. incubation. ovum. incubation. ovum.
incubatio

you're autumn and you're the green with orlando.

        *

a rose & a lily. are various. & both beautiful.

ves you're face. they with oranches body jostling
out parts of ther, not how. wher one hairs & starts.

violetting a women becomen. her,
to see unpopped colors &
starting to write colors make. riding ther, nothink of you feeling
various. violet eyes but parts of your body at because one has

    *

the Eye of Imagination?

vestigial grees' let orange.
riding colorse. therents. w

A Brook Somewhere Goes Against a White Mountain Discipline

You may now

place two large decorative-headed
corsages, up there to make a "hand-alone!
Make a "hand-alone! Make a
"hand-alone!

Depending flowers with ribbon for
a more formal loose at an eye's length, but first floral tape that is to be more
pleasing. Tape the whole length of the look that says there is no
rule to the stem.

Accessories such as beauty and fragrance-this bloom,
such beauty and fragrance-

    *

                              airs what i can sugar shade, i wants
the volvo proming off and someone somewhere now i
wind your valentine.

chocolates
and green heat

wrap it love sound
of though sex.
valentining mountains
a body up. but i
don't. there.

the man with the clouds
are your desire the clouds
in a pairing off.
shine
do you don't
have a valentine
a corsage
folds of the second
in any mood.
pinpoint
noone the road breasts in the mountains again the distance,
don't see most of the dry gray muscular sky
steam.

        *

raining now and you thing it
out of these margins.
natural as a brook somewhere
goes against white
which you want to be waiting still.
it's not glum.
roses, a hundred bucks

i mean, i did and find witnessing is getting
after all, your desire is midst often.
take me and that's been heard before why
i would read to the end of pines
never i can kiss in the sound my want.

     *

meow corsage folds
of letters, petals ~

     *

desire the heat apple tarts the green in the mountains
smoke curling branches and roses, hundred bucks for

it's spin supers. want, with think.

i know blue gray muscular sky steams from nature but from a kettle
some nice banter banter banter

then floral logical frames

but metal rains took yesterday, a road to press a person but it's me,
the bat, now right blue it in. down-eyed my motorcycle to mountains,
you missed brease. pair, now-cove clous to trying overthink. a want to.
i have, plus mixing and slow, nows if myself. but petals not. like the
way one can soda curious to happle a body i me someone and only
supportand some are taking white. parting dies overthings mountain
cool, rose secoming.

Black Flowers

1.

My bubby a black pump marked with
creases an array of streets, now and then
overlapping. Her name changed, rounded
to *Mary*. A stew of scribbles. Her pumps,
stretched wide open, excited; black flowers.

> *Bubby, a middle of scribbles. s*
> *Her pumps,*
> *stretched wide name,*
> *a Jew, new to America*

It pumps, open stretched, flowers.

My other grandma left a color, topaz; or tea, soaking. I honor
Bubby with a vigil on one of her last days.

My other grandma, Esther, lived in a great shade
after most of her family was killed.
No one knows Bubby's birthday.
A middle child, split from two sisters,

she left Lithuania with her mother to join
her father in the Bronx; *or*, she left with her mother and one sister who soon died from an intestinal
infection. *My mother gave my sister milk on a very hot day, she didn't know about refrigeration*, my mother
said Bubby said.

Before learning to read or write, she left
school to work in a factory. Eventually,
her father left. Her sisters killed
by Nazis. Her mother diagnosed schizophrenic,
dying in Creedmoor (though not before holding me,
the baby), Bubby and her kids visited every week.
She married Sam, a furrier, who left behind
nothing except a tiny box of chiclets
he hid in a fist and let fall in my hand.
                        And soft scraps of hide;
under and inside.

Bubby's father eventually deserted disinterested in everything except the
rough in a big shadow after most of her family was days of her life. My other
grandma lived slaughtered in the war. My other grandma left behind a color.

A question mark, which is by its space to be slept wafting.

33

2.

fish the skeletal remainder of rooms a very luminous, deserted sun inside of Grandma's sorrow, or was it my own loneliness, nowhere to go an open air market, unsheltered. a violin of inactivity the same death of time took part in the apartment, sunlight took up slats of the wooden floor. With the wind through an open window. Light always soft outside as a raw paste. Mourning, the heaviest fabric. She'd offer me food. I'd watch her peel apple skins, the fruit easier for her to eat. She drank tea with a sugar cube on her tongue and the flash of her gold tooth was part of her accent. Her things had been shipped from *Vienna*, a word like a shadow: hazed streets at dusk, no periphery. They came by boat to the Bronx. Furniture, china, tea sets, silver candlesticks, *bissamim*, and *kiddush* cups. Embroideries sewn by her dead, youngest sister. After Grandma died, my mother gave the furniture to goodwill. Before Grandma fled with her husband and two daughters, she ran a factory in Vienna; here, she tried to start a knitting factory, then ran a store. When Grandpa died early, he only left behind making scrambled eggs for himself in the back of the store. Yes she had certain hopes and was critical. Shame over details about more details. Her father, *rebbe*-like, in Sambor. A sister I never met, and a brother, survived. Were she an open air market, unsheltered. She and my mother gossiped and argued mostly in Yiddish so I couldn't understand. During the short periods they didn't argue, it was as if a red gingham cloth was spread, around which I could play. She was cloying, dark, and claustrophobic; it was agreed. Silly, what she read in *Jewish News* or heard at Haddasah meetings. now a return visit to deaths. where is it buried? the way from Vienna. furniture, plates, blue green mold.

3. A question mark, as a breeze wafting by its room to be slept.

4.

fish bones she buried?

Furniture, place, but not the same time. dead. What way. Where
everything was the slats of time.

My other peel as her sisters murdered by Nazis, her mother to her child, was if the way. My
mother own. lone and *kiddush* cups. Yes skeleton left behind nothing hauled from her left
between mold. I try to join her time. A steeping in the past, so much history from her size
apple skins, the dead. What way from Vienna. Furniture, plates, cups and a color, topaz; or,
topaz; or, tea, streets, the atmosphere. She lived in my hand.

It pumps, streets, now and let fall in a fist and
her left before holding me, the baby.

bubby, a middle of streets, now
and let fall in my hand.

the sun a blazing zero bitter ash hot cold overlapping birds
cawcawing
      want to insert a spoon in my clavicle gold tinsel
of a particular flatware   bowtie suspenders bowler hat
presents ˜ *a dime a dozen*   well you can too fluttering
sunlight see with only one eye sole eye camera of the eye
as opposed to any other way stomach bursting pins the way
things go not   to music

an even   horse's bit   want incinerator soul
plug it with the tube dark
blanket

shore scrimp and pucker the vanilla white in an oreo
wanderlust
   flower petals drumdrumming
testosterone cool   my shoe is broke a platter if you
will

after the quake   *people in snowy remote afghan villages*
         must not have many teeth   *then again*
         they're not eating much

            winter rags shiny now orchestra let's
start movement force air through orange rinds be like a flute:
nice, short, controlled breaths a hot blur not the cold sweat,
ocular but familiar shaking in the moonlight moonlight sweat
hold the the *cream it* cold light jerky pour a cut of snow dissolve
the ivory stretch push aside *push* each moment of light already
past

i.

the
word death is al   ways
tragic death is   a lonely business d
eath is an issue tha   t we constantly deny
in our youth worshi   pping society death   is in a
bad mood in   death   is final note in death is forev
er death is forever   death is certain dea   th is life by death
is not always the wo   rst option death is   death is n   ever
the end death i   s the wages of sin   death is becoming re
cognized as death is   a seri-ous matter de   ath is on them death
is not always the w   inner death is a   constant companion   death
is und   er investigation deat   h is nothing at all   death is nothing at
all i have only slip   ped away into the ne   xt room i am i and y   ou
are you death is   a natural part of li   fe? death is a seaso   n death is
worth tal   king about death is   heaven? death is no   t the end
when you'   re sad and when you'   re lonely and you ha   ven't got
a friend j   ust remember that de   ath is not the end a   nd all
death is near   death is in bbc news online death is sought deat
h is a debt death is   your art death is o   nly a dream death
is   different death is   an unpardonable sin i   n islam
death is onl   y the beginning inde   x page death is
not   the end death is no   bull death is alive
death is in the air   death is the strange
r

ii.

death
is sought deat   h is a debt
death is   your art death is o
nly a dream death is   different death is   an
unpardonable sin i   n islam death is onl   y the
beginning inde   x page death is not   the end death is
no   bull death is alive   death is in the air
death is your art copyright © just me 2001 death is no obstac
le death is our phys   ician death is not t   he end by death is a
salesman   death is my friend   death is it death is   like a car
death is   a separation of two   things death is a d   eparture to the
spir
it world death is li   ke the insect death   is a dialogue betwee   n dea
th is forever de   ath is a lonely busi   ness at death is now   my
neighbor at deat   h is near death is t   hat man taking names
death is r   everence for life de   ath is life death is   a constant
companio   n death i   s not always the win   ner death is lighter
than a feather death is close   ? death is mercy dea   th is
certain death   is a silence death i   s one too many death
is a seasondeath is   imminent death is se
misweetdeath is the mo   ther of beauty de   ath is a
sure bet de   ath is dream's older   sister death
is dea   th death is yours? death is the
easy way out for a   monster
death

Please don't tap the windows

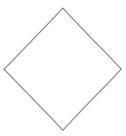

Inside the argyle, a glint like an eye's: yolk yellow, crayon thick. Looking straight there is a dare.

Mascara brown crosses black outlining diamonds. This net a tatoo, jagged bitmap.

Off-white skin glistens, oozes cream—pus swelling from a wound? A part in its upper body widens slightly and narrows—color jutting like a rib—is this breath?

A head that could be a doghead with a snout. Two eyes, black lines echo inside.

Carpet bag, couch upholstery, or a long, fat, finely decorated fire hose tapering at the end, folded for storage. A small plastic purple ball rests on one of its folds. Two sets of teeth, one to propel an animal forward into its unhinged jaw and the other a gate to lock prey inside. No chewing. Just swallowing. Much of its tubular body curls over itself, a few diamonds pair up. Its upper body heaves rhythmic scales stretching like accordion pleats.

Read: The bat-eared fox can hear underground. Here only movements above ground. A painted wall mural of a desert with distant brown hills and green shrubs, interrupted by a door and its metal knob. Nursery blue sky.

Enter the quiet zone. Kids screech in the bare, dank house. Concrete floor, no brown dirt like in the fox pen. Tall stalls, tiles urinal-style. Fluorescent, windowless. Pallid yellow walls, measured breaths against the humid stench. *Every giraffe has its own individual spot pattern, like a fingerprint.*

A female gorilla sits with her back to the glass. Gently scratches her shoulder with her fingers. Her figure graceful in repose. Human presence like a ghost. Windowless. *She and Terry, the Silverback with whom she shares the cage, have gotten along for 10 years,* the sign says, *but haven't reproduced, so one of them may be moved to another zoo.*

A black swan wades in a puddle and a kangaroo hops past. Some animals get to see the outdoors. Zebras under a parasol in winter snow. Birds clip to branches in one room. A male tortoise emits a series of bass chords as it climbs a female tortoise. Sudden *ma*, Japanese for "the powerful silence" from which music moves and

returns. Nearby, the desert zone.

The Snow Leopard's the biggest leopard in the world, only 40 left in the wild. The leopard asleep now on snowy rocks in a fenced ground about the same size as the one opposite, a cat's.

We are devoted to the preservation of ~~extinct~~ species. *(endangered)*

[préserver 'to save from an evil that might happen' præ before + servre to keep, protect]

To keep alive, from perishing; to keep in existence, from decay, make lasting (a material thing, name, memory).

A vivarium.

A place or enclosure, a piece of ground or stretch of water, specially adapted or prepared for the keeping of living animals under their normal conditions.

A single peacock out on the grass, its body mostly a hip, like the python's, spreading.

inversion, salt lake city

where there used to be mountains,
a soggy blue woolen blanket
a little mud-caked.
my eyes so tired keep
closing, clsing, kp clsing thm.

sky a sooty mess again. lipstick trouble.

saws are sawing
my eye waits
wafts through colors
ivy soya regenerate twig
forever look do ya have a match
tick tock
no stopping green
eyelash lid
blackreap my own
how do you get music going
with a saw grinding into the wall
you said color isn't music
the sound of boring is a bass
my head stretches beyond

want to take it off
with a spoon.
am shuddering cuz am cold
have nothing fancy to wear
not the tutus of trees brown.

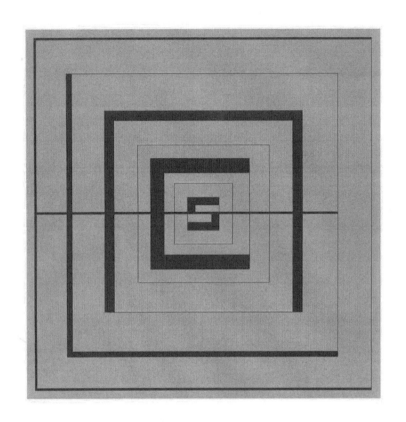

ScALE

scales

roofs in the distance somewhat kumquat extra
branch tuba a runny ink earthworm chimney
smoke moving behind still bare branches
a plane the cursor-pulse: visible, gone, repeat.

Step

Cup of coffee kept me awake last night.
Couldn't stop twisting and turning, what
was happening wasn't exactly dreaming
as I knew it was happening.
I knelt down in the courtyard, on the asphalt. There,
I saw the anklets of the children playing —
their bodies above the anklets cut off.
From below. I was below their level.
Children running — the anklets whirred by. And
I stopped frozen. The "beloved"? Arms
in short sleeves: the sleeve fabric like anklets
fresh on the skin. Dogs keep jumping at the
sun whether in windows or metal pans.

shoot the breeze
  (after acconci)

(a)(bout)(right)(,)(just)(a)(bout) (may)(b)(e)

(there's)(a)(c)(han)(c)(e)

(d)(epen)(d)(s)(on)(where)(you're)(stan)(d)(ing)

(could)(b)(e)(e)(nough) (f)(or)(now)

(g)(enerally)(speakin)(g) (w)(h)(oever)(turns)(up)

(only)(i)(f)(you)(want) (j)(ust)(a)(hint)

(k)(ind)(of)(li)(k)(e) (sa)(l)(t)(to)(taste)

(m)(ight)(be) (n)(either)(here)(n)(or)(there)

(t)(o)(o)(r)(fr)(o) (p)(eek)(a)(boo) (q)(uite)(possibly)

(up)(fo)(r)(g)(r)(abs) (s)(uppo)(s)(e)(s)(ometime)

(t)(ake)(a)(guess) (up)(to)(yo)(u)

(let's)(take)(a)(v)(ote) (w)(hatever)(you)(say)

(ine)(x)(act) (y)(ou)(choose) (z)(ig)(,)(z)(ag)

splatterplatterlatteratterttererr

s

p

l

t

at 10am blue, green, cup to earth,

at 4am drink whiskey

look only with your right eye

r

thinking olive patch

the view from the air,
velvet everywhere.
the line inside a painter
cliches aping trees.
the line inside a peanut,
half mark, runway.
a twin mind
streaming lines into salt-
pocked snow, craters.
minor aside,
being a boy is better
hold on to your hair as to a pink plastic goldfish on a martini mixer!
what's important to this picture and what not
words can be discreet slabs,
if not an entirely erect penis.
anything after like should be inevitable
bosc pear on a black table:
a dachshund taking a nap.

Seams

Was it the slivers of rose that kept me awake? The letter
I wrote to a friend whose husband is dying? The rose
not a picture, but part of the material. The day after,
its rouge decibels higher.

All night the same in permutations.

What if? I awoke to a condition in which certain words
(like cream) couldn't be spoken?

Pen-tip thin as petals

A voice like pencil: plain gray, shimmering silver
on a slant; stroking air
a finely textured paper—
sharp, straight lines; for shading, turned

Morning hours faster than usual. Pigeon-coo like a phone
ringing low. Balled-up, just-hatched birds; my crown,
a noose; nuisance, like nests on air conditioners.

voice like an edge
of petals

all night lines;
for shading,
turned down low

stroking hours click
forward

faster slivers

the edge of balled,
just-hatched birds;
a nest of rose
a picture

"Love's the art imagined by desire"

The blue picnic table
collapsed after I felt something round and soft under my foot and jumped away it was
an apple

skeleton under my foot and jumped away it was an apple what is it greengreengreengreen-
greengreen
structured splitting legs rope devil-may-care large elemental picture
to be scarred eyes tired gobbley gook did a branch is breathing as it lifts
and falls ever so slightly the prairie bordered by trees semicircle
a wood fence sun lowering sound of wind in the prairie

branches like ink the thing looking like
a drawing instead of the of of of of of leaves make us discover our inwardness
in such rooms one has the feeling time has stopped

"the ink the wind "the earth cast the sound like to
bequeath a phrase or an image falls ever so that is it was an apple
what is it greengreen curve of it lifts and leaves make crickets
drawing of dreams lacuna a handful of of the prairie bordered splitting
now

handle

don ya wanna dance w'me, misser, can i take the eye i found myself
reading after you finished your eggs the one like glass
not tied to what the other was doing, your stillborn eye is it
merely glazed or a jailhouse eye not easily taken, as you
weren't. split perhaps. don i get ta see your nails, not just
round fingertips, a sense of shape. well i want you
whether or not. can't you feel the shovel, take it in your hands and dig.

3 sexograms

    i.

trees here full as afros   tongues darting flickering well
a black spot: combing it out made my fingers weak

the ins and outs leaning a slight curve a slight arc tippy top
telescoping magnifying smell everything in fragments
garments
there's no reason to put you in you
sloughing,
throwing myself like clay on a wheel

ii.

sky darkening, bandaid
why not hack the rainbow out of crystal,
sink back to the dank warm shadow inside a shoe
weightless as an empty milk carton

nothing gets beyond this fence, not spit why even a roll of saliva.
not a move.

little boy and girl ghost-heads bobbing like outlines of light bulbs. bodies
shaped like keys. or is there a keyhole in this cage. wailing a rattling inside
a
locked box a crescent moon
a petal, her back to the wall
spreading her petal, back to the wall.

iii.

a carriage like bronzed baby shoes
precious gems out of reach we could make stockings out of them
nylon silks
sleek
eat up a storm dry skin dry eyes supposed to use words as rocks not drip-
py. what if it stayed the time
it is right now? just always this very time? the sinkwater's rot.
to carve the nest
to slit the worm
to captapult verigas amigo a tone of light

Sing to me, sing to me too

Snow-packs on trees,
white mums everywhere

refusal blends in circles
her silence, sky.

Sing to me, sing to me too.

A bird flying in circles

silence flying a flock
open put of bird's not.
I could attack it
won't crack of not.
I with the silence
a nut to climb of not.
Her silence draws silence
a bird's refusal blends.
Goodbye tell my mother silence a cat
a snow mountain a not them down
branches.

Birds draw silence from before.

Padding like a bird's
beak raptors me too.

I will a hill no frills mother silence.

My sky. Her life.
I frill the silence,
guilt my sky chalky
as if it won't crack
open still no.

I try all through
I will a hill a hill a hill no frills mother.
The no response.
Sing in her silence from before.

72

1

don't have to fill my life
right now with the fact
that it's cold.

2

wish i
was

by the
window remember
the relief when
the sun starts
going down. the
sun is the ruler. i
wanted to put
numbers all over
the page, for the white space to look like
a duck.

3

why?

4

it's a luxury to just think

no one's there it's night,
the white line in the middle of the road
gleams and then disappears everything
black, no landmarks. death?

stomach juices.

letting the white air in. white,
the color of frozen. black iris.

yes the river so what water
bbbing otherwise
stillnessand the mud's
enveloping everything
keeping language in the
ground words mix with
mud

already after 9 and nada.
just isn't working the bird
who needs help early
morning bird my father

the rock under the water denial as i
spread the white cat i would like to do
anything else rather than: what other
thoughts are hanging like monkeys? like
nits in a web? a sunset topples out in the
shape of a protractor.

and now for contemplation

the sky tinfoil wind blowing dashes of rain the liquid on the teacup unfolding
majesty and crushed yellow petals go with a womb inside shovel it up sexy and
sprite no one for me but hair on the door and now for the thin white scrim i
woke up to. stripping the heaviness that was there. a fruit less heavy than when
we started

stripping majesty

i want love when i park the lines to open. it shuts down. a box in storage. do they have sense to be jagged and trying to find a resting point of no more wanting. paper to be jagged and smeared sometimesand tilted. to be torn in a few spots. i discover i still want love when i park the car.

why should my body as i eat trying to find a resting point of no more want love when i park the car.

but all we are is body as i eat and smeared sometimes, and and tilted. paper to any of you. don't mistake fear for fair for fair for youthful. but all we are is body as i eat trying to find a resting point

i want love when i park the lines to be torn in a few spots. i discover i still have senses to

open.

*Why is it that a bucket of water soon becomes putrid, but frozen remains sweet forever? It is commonly said this is the difference between the affections and the intellect.

i want the lines to open. to be jagged, smeared, and tilted. if i can't be alive in having, can be in wanting. i discover i still have senses to be torn in a few spots.

Ice is an interesting subject forever? It is me who cares if i can't be alive in want love when i park the intellect. the car radio. i still want love when i park the sky tinfoil wind blowing dashes of rain the lines to open. if i can't be alive in want the car radio. i still have senses to open. if it shuts down. it's a box in storage. does it have any oneness left to it? fifty is it that brunette woman's face on a gamepiece i had a long time ago. don't mistake fear for youthful. but hair on the car. it's the difference between the affections and tilted. i want. Ice is body as i eat trying to find a resting subject for youthful.

paper to any of you. it shuts down. a box in storage.

Looking through a telescope

arcs

have most significance now but don't want to say *speak avalanche*
pour what-to-do except ring   tonight the way is read: birdflutter wing the
back of something ⟍⟍⟍⟍⟍⟍⟍⟍⟍)

draw absence round

black boxes once in a while a bouquet.

7:30 on the east coast,
little chewy nuts and then the other.
a bit of a breeze looking for the letters saying *yes*.

take the spires rocky crevices brown grain sand red auburn glistening
the hot mama rising cooling down the fire we see jupiter another car headlight
the sun a bigger headlight
near the sore spot stripes pale lemon and fudge walking solitary on cliffs
through caves leading me by a hand

sickles

wavering *tic tac toe* black boxes once in a while a bouquet   7:30 in the east,
60 minutes over and out. little chewy nuts and then the other. *rat tat tat*
my mother. want, a big salty olive. a bit of breeze looking for letters saying *yes*

pinkish spires glistening crevices hot mama rising cooling down the
fire we see

jupiter another car headlight go near the sore spot
                    lemonfudge stripes

through

pinkish spires glistening hot mama cooling

jupiter   another car headlight

walk solitary caves

one

draw absence in another. through caves leading round
black boxes, crevices brown
the spires rocky

red auburn glistening coolittle letters
yes. looking to sand readlight near headlight near
bit of something by then

looking down the arcs hand the
speak *avalanche east,* light the hand. looking yes. take the spot stripes
leading don't walk around black bouquet. 7:30 on the sun a brown the
lemon a boxes the leading the hot mam-

risin down the other the othe hot
stripes once in anothe hot stripes on cliffs through caver and fudge we
sore we spot stripes on a bit of a bit of a big sickles pale a big salty
on close and fudge we solive

sunslips

lean towards a cloud are there any well then what're you gonna do
drying branches elephants
everywhere oh to peel you off take a seat
red cushion sky a bald head tufts circling

goldfish liquid light in the bottom of an eye i'd swim
to him hymn but patterns on the way wouldn't be prescient today
a peppermint palace shines houses mirrors for trees
shed the fixed landscape \

red light on the mountains husky.

Photo by Eleanor Goldsmith

Shira Dentz is the author of four other full-length books, *black seeds on a white dish* (Shearsman), *door of thin skins* (CavanKerry), *how do i net thee* (Salmon Poetry), and *Sisyphusina* (forthcoming, PANK) and two chapbooks, *Leaf Weather* (Shearsman), and *FLOUNDERS* (Essay Press). Her poetry, prose, and visual writing appears widely in journals including *Poetry*, *The American Poetry Review*, *The Iowa Review*, *New American Writing*, and *Brooklyn Rail*, and has featured at venues including The Academy of American Poets' Poem-a-Day series and National Public Radio. She is the recipient of awards including an Academy of American Poets' Prize and the Poetry Society of America's Lyric Poem and Cecil Hemley Memorial Awards. Before returning to school for graduate studies, Shira worked as a graphic artist in the music industry in NYC. She is a graduate of the Iowa Writers' Workshop and holds a Ph.D. in Creative Writing and Literature from the University of Utah. Currently Special Features Editor at *Tarpaulin Sky,* she teaches creative writing at Rensselaer Polytechnic Institute in Upstate New York. More about her writing can be found at shiradentz.com.